Instructions for using AR

LET AUGMENTED REALITY CHANGE HOW YOU READ A BOOK

With your smartphone, iPad or tablet you can use the **Hasmark AR** app to invoke the augmented reality experience to literally read outside the book.

1. Download the **Hasmark app** from the **Apple App Store** or **Google Play**

2. Open and select the (vue) option

3. Point your lens at the full image with the and enjoy the augmented reality experience.

Go ahead and try it right now with the Hasmark Publishing International logo.

ENDORSEMENTS

"If you have ever needed a little help along the way to achieve your dreams, Mina's words will certainly resonate with you and you will be able to instantly translate her message into action."

—Judy O'Beirn,
President of Hasmark Publishing International

"Start With Me! Who Am I?: Discovering Yourself With The Law Of Attraction will inspire you to explore your inner world from a place of higher truth. Mina's message is practical, spiritual, kind, and clear. This is a must-read book for anyone who is ready to experience the power of transformation from a place of Love. It will change the way you think and feel, but ultimately, your way of being. It was a wonderful experience to have met Mina Vo! Her wisdom and loving presence reflect her commitment to changing lives!"

—Valeria T. Koopman,
founder of Fit For Joy, Healing Books author, and
host of *A Quest for Well-Being podcast.*
www.fitforjoy.org

"If it essential for growth to develop the depth of understanding as Mina Vo brilliantly shares in her book Start With Me. You will discover that the flow of this book is designed to inspire you to express your greatness and to experience the gifts this life has to offer."

—Peggy McColl,
New York Times Bestselling Author,
http://PeggyMcColl.com

START WITH ME!

WHO AM I?

Discovering YOURSELF with the Law of Attraction

Mina Vo

Hasmark Publishing www.hasmarkpublishing.com
Copyright © 2022 Mina Vo
First Edition

Disclaimer
This book is designed to provide information and motivation to our readers. It is sold with the understanding that the publisher is not engaged to render any type of psychological, legal, or any other kind of professional advice. The content of each article is the sole expression and opinion of its author, and not necessarily that of the publisher. No warranties or guarantees are expressed or implied by the publisher's choice to include any of the content in this volume. Neither the publisher nor the individual author(s) shall be liable for any physical, psychological, emotional, financial, or commercial damages, including, but not limited to, special, incidental, consequential or other damages. Our views and rights are the same: You are responsible for your own choices, actions, and results. Permission should be addressed in writing to Mina Vo at info@minavocoaching.com

Editor: Harshita Sharma harshita@hasmarkpublishing.com
Cover Design: Anne Karklins anne@hasmarkpublishing.com
Interior Layout: Amit Dey amit@hasmarkpublishing.com

ISBN 13: 978-1-77482-160-2
ISBN 10: 1774821605

DEDICATION

*To my husband, Claude, for guiding me and supporting
me along my journey with him.*

*To my three young adults, Mylène, Alexis, and Raphaël,
who are my inspirations and encouragement in my life.*

TABLE OF CONTENTS

CHAPTER 1

RECOGNIZING WHO I AM

"I am who I am. Not who you think I am. Not who you want me to be. I am me."

—Brigitte Nicole

There are a lot of people wanting to become financially free, have a good life, have no stress, and have the freedom to choose and do what they want in life, but very few of them know how to plan to get what they want. Well, I can tell you that you are holding in your hands the road map to find the **essence** of who you are so that you can adjust yourself to get what you want in life. No goal setting is effective unless you know **who you are** and **what you want**. To get what you want, you must know who you are and be conscious of where you come from, your purpose in life, your paradigm—and the only way to be aware of what you want is to start within yourself.

Who am I? Do I only have one identity or more? Is there more than one form in me? It must be since I have my soul, which is the non-physical form, my spiritual guidance, and me in physical form with bone and flesh.

I am composed of a physical being and a non-physical being (my soul or inner being) and thus, they are inseparable from each other. I am part of the divine, like the branches that are part of the vine. I cannot pinch myself off from my inner being, my soul. It is my divine self, and I am the one who cocreates with my divine self to make things become reality.

Everything that exists on this planet Earth was created more than once. It has to be visualized, dreamed of, and finalized. It needs the action from the physical form and the thinking of the non-physical form to make things a reality.

Think about it for a moment: before you were born, you were imagined first by your parents when they had a desire to make a child or children. Their desire was manifested when they were in a moment of ecstasy about their love for each other, and the union of the energy from the strongest sperm with the right timing of the creation of the woman's egg created a synergy at that moment, and impregnation happened. Can you imagine that? You were formed from a single cell, during a period of nine months (approximately 268 days on an average, according to *Wikipedia*) for the gestation period, when all the cells in your body were multiplying, organizing, and forming a beautiful human being like YOU! It takes time, patience, and energy to be created, and none of us were born on this planet accidentally. We are chosen and we are here with a purpose, with a mission. We were very happy and eager before we came to this planet Earth. We were eager to cocreate with other human beings. Each of us is unique and born with a purpose and a desire to cocreate, be free, and enjoy life on this beautiful planet, the Earth.

You see, the human being is the only species that takes at least eighteen plus years to become totally independent. There are always exceptions, of course. The other species on this planet become independent much faster than us. Look at a horse, a dog, or a cat—their babies can crawl, walk, and know how to find food in just a few hours or days after they have been born. This is probably due to their short lifespan. They don't have time to lose, and their brains do not have to develop as much as the human brain; therefore, no need to wait, evolution has made it so.

We are an image of God, the Tao, or the Universe, whichever you want to call a creator. We cocreate with each other to make this world better to live in. If we are an image of God, the creator, then everything we can create is and will be the creations in collaboration with God or the Universe, right?

Since we are an image of God, then what we say, think, feel, and react should be a God-like image, don't you think so? I believe so. If I want to speak, think, sense, and respond like God, then, first of all, I better examine myself and start to know myself first—to know who I am and what I want to do, feel, and experiment with on this planet Earth with other human beings.

Why start with me? If I want to contribute to the changing of the world, I have to **start the change in myself first**, and to do that, I've got to know how to start the change in my cells.

There are over 35 trillion cells in your body; luckily, they are working harmoniously with each other to keep you alive every millisecond. It's a beautiful army that you demand a lot from, sometimes. They work on automation most of the time and have antennas on each of them so that they communicate effectively according to your program unless you are conscious to command them to react differently. Each one of them is very adaptable and very smart. They can change instantly with your consciousness that controls and commands them.

Whatever your command is, your cells obey without questioning—they just do what you want them to do.

They can kill each other slowly every day if you permit them to by thinking about negative thoughts, and your permission is unconscious because of the program that runs in you.

So, in order to reprogram your thinking or habit (your paradigm), you've got to be conscious of your thoughts, emotions, feelings, reactions, and actions. Thoughts lead to emotion, emotion to feeling, feeling to reaction, and reaction to action. Action has two ways to go:

1. The wanted way, or
2. The unwanted way.

Either way, you must feel good about your choice. That will help you to position yourself to receive what you want in life.

REFLECTION: Recognize who you are.

Answer these questions:

1. **WHAT** is the only thing I really want at this moment of time in my life?

____

____

____

____

____

2. **WHY** do I want it? What's in it for me?

3. What do I need to **KNOW** or **LEARN** in order to get what I want?

4. **WHO** can cocreate with me in this process of wanting?

5. **HOW** can I do it? What are the steps that I need to plan in order to get to what I want?

6. **WHEN** do I want to realize my goal? (Put deadlines to the steps that you have written in #5. Break them down into smaller steps if you need to.)

STEPS	WHO CAN HELP ME GET WHAT I WANT FOR THIS STEP? (Name)	WHEN DO I WANT IT TO BE DONE? (Date)
1		
2		
3		
4		
5		
6		

7. Take a look at what you have written from 1–6 and say it aloud in the morning after waking up and at night before going to bed and FEEL that you've already gotten what you want. Do this for thirty days so that it registers into your subconscious. The Law of Attraction will slowly bring you what you want when you are ready to position yourself to receive it. Somehow, the repeating and feeling of what you intend to have initiates the attraction in all components; either opportunities or people with whom you want to cocreate will come to you from nowhere.

Don't forget to do it with a sense of service and purpose.

CHAPTER II

KNOWING MYSELF FIRST

"You can conquer almost any fear if you will only make up your mind to do so. For remember, fear doesn't exist anywhere except in the mind."

—Dale Carnegie

Why do I have to know myself first? Well, if I want to create a great relationship with anybody or anything in this world, isn't it more plausible that I should know about myself first? If I don't know myself well enough, how can I possibly express myself so others can understand me to cocreate with me? And thus, how can I expect others to perceive me as I want them to?

A good relationship with anyone depends on my ability and knowledge of that person. How can I create a great relationship if I don't know about the person I am interacting with? If I want to know the person well, I must first know myself well in order to communicate my needs. If I cannot communicate my needs well enough, then I cannot expect the other person to understand me well since I am unable to tell him/her what I want.

What do I want from this relationship? How can I bring happiness to this person and vice versa? We are attracted to each other because we complement the needs of each other, either at work or at home. We are a social species and need each other for our survival in the long term. No one can survive for the long term if he/she is standing alone and has no interaction with anybody. We need to interact with each other for our survival by being in the relationship and gathering in the community. It all starts with a relationship between two or more persons at a time.

Imagine two lovers: if they want to build a great relationship with each other, they have a lot of questions to ask each other the first time they meet, right? One person wants to know as much as possible about the other person in order to adjust to his/her vibration, trying to match with that other person as much as possible if they feel the right vibe.

In order to create a great relationship with anyone, I have to create a great relationship with MYSELF first, and to do that, I have to **know myself** inside out. I've got to know my why, my purpose, my goal, and what I love. What is my level of self-confidence? And most of all, what do I want?

How to know about myself? I ask myself these questions:

FIRST:

What is my *why*?

Why am I doing what I am doing right now?

What are the reasons for my existence?

Who do I live for?

What is my *purpose* in life?

SECOND:

What is my *goal*?

What do I want from life?

What am I ready to give in order to receive what I want from life in exchange?

Who do I want to be right now?

Who do I want to become in one year from now?

THIRD:

What do I *love* to do and who do I *want* to be? (For example: I want to travel around the world and live in an abundance of financial freedom, etc.)

What is my level of *self-confidence* to do it?

Do I want to do it alone or with someone else?

Do I want to become such and such a person?

I just need to know *what I want*!

REFLECTION: How to know about yourself?

Take time to answer the above questions. They help you to know more about yourself and what you want.

____

____

____

____

____

____

Now that you know about your why, goal, and what you love or want, how do you feel about yourself? Your level of self-confidence depends on the level of your knowledge about the subject in question. The more you know about your subject, the more confident you are to talk about it.

That means the more you know about yourself, the more confident you can be in expressing your feelings about what you want, who you want to be, and who you want to hang out with, eventually knowing how to put yourself into a **flexible mindset** so that **you can manifest what you want** and really enjoy life to the maximum.

Knowing yourself deep down means being **conscious of what you want** and especially what you want to manifest in your life. Self-confidence is built with knowledge, and knowledge together with action is power! Thus, knowledge about yourself and others puts you in control of any situations in relation to others. So, knowing who you are and what you want first will help you to spread that energy of confidence about yourself. What does that bring to you? The same energy of confidence from your surroundings, from the people you encounter, from things and events that are attracted to your life with the same vibrational energy frequencies that you project out into the world. What you put out there will come back to you. That's the Law of Action and Reaction.

What you think and what you feel, you attract the same from others since thoughts are emitted into the environment by vibrations and frequencies. When the frequency of your thought meets another frequency similar to it, it emphasizes and creates synergy or momentum, either good or bad.

So, when you don't appreciate yourself, you don't love yourself, you are ashamed of yourself, or even when you don't like or love such and such a person, what happens is you are on the frequency of hate, comparison, and frustration, which are at lower levels of vibrational frequency on Abraham-Hicks' emotional scale (Fig. 1). Then what happens is that you attract more of those feelings from people who've got the same frequencies in your environment, and that's why some days you feel it is a bad day for you—that's because you are the one who attracts it unknowingly.

The only way to get out of that emotion is to love others as you love yourself, as Jesus taught us. That way, when you put yourself in the happy and love frequencies, you will then only attract love, appreciation, and compassion from others, which eventually help you get into that high vibrational energy and upgrade your relationship with others.

Knowing yourself first helps you to be conscious of your feelings and emotions. You are in a proactive mode instead of a reactive mode. You know that everything happens to you because you attract it to your life. So, if you want to attract goodness in others, you have to think about goodness from others, even the ones who bother you, who hate you, who you hate, and who you don't appreciate. That's how the Law of Attraction works. By doing so, you put yourself in a position to receive what you've asked for.

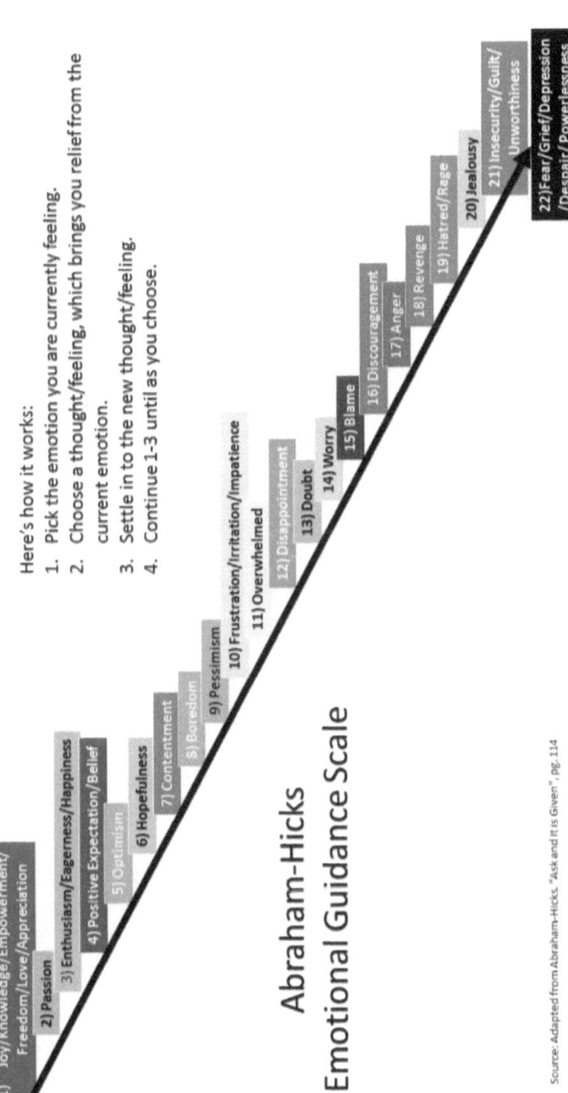

Fig. 1: Abraham-Hicks, Emotional Guidance Scale. From 365 Days in Aspen, blog Ups and Downs. *(Published Jan. 15, 2017, by Brownell Landrum.)*

CHAPTER III

THE LAW OF ATTRACTION AND ME

*"When you JUDGE others, you do not define them.
You define YOURSELF."*

—Earl Nightingale

What is the Law of Attraction? It's a universal law that works like the law of gravity. For me, the law of gravity is physics, while the Law of Attraction is quantum physics. The Law of Attraction works with our feelings, emotions, vibrations, and energy. We know that the law of gravity exists; that's why nobody wants to jump from an airplane without a parachute because we know that the person would be dead meat in a few seconds. That's how the law of gravity works, doesn't it?

Well, the Law of Attraction works in the same manner. Whatever we *feel*, we are attracting, either good or bad. By the way, "good" or "bad" are only perceptions. The same event could be "good" for one person and "bad" for another. Take an example of a pickpocket. If he has successfully picked someone's wallet, then for him, he has a good day, but it's a bad day for the person who has been robbed, isn't it? Thus, it is the same event with the same action, only different perceptions depending on where you observe it from. Your angle of observation depends on where your position is relative to the object, person, or thing that you are observing. A different angle gives you a different perception of the object or person that you are looking at.

We automatically associate new learnings with what we have already learned and stored in our subconscious mind. If we are conscious of this association, we can be aware and selective and can decide whether or not to store the new information as it is or do some *reflection* on it before storing it. If we are not conscious, then the new information is associated with the old information and stored automatically as a "true" fact. But "true" or "false" depends on the angle of perception from which we observe the subject.

Take a look at the following photos. Depending on what angle you are looking at the hand, your association of his hand's gesture has a different meaning.

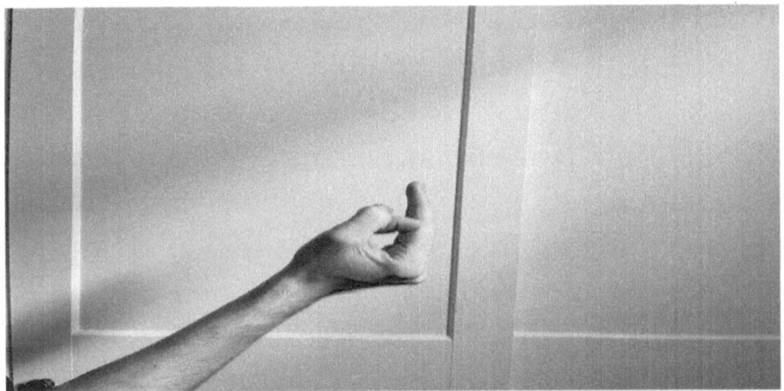

Profile view

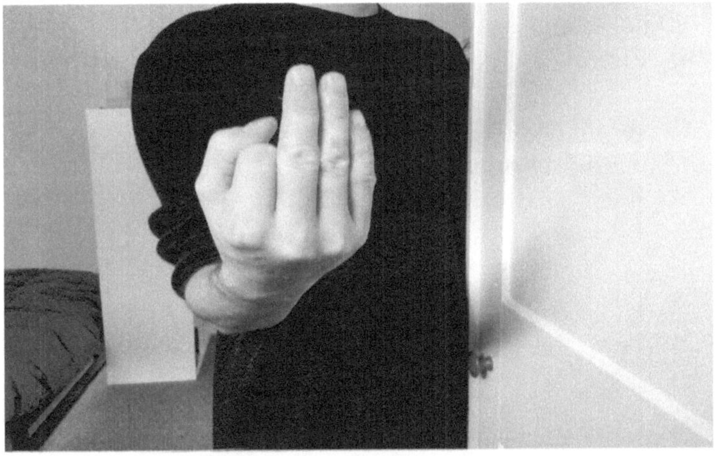

Front view

Thus, our interpretation of the world depends on the angle of perception from where we observe the fact, and also, it mostly depends on our mindset, our programmed paradigm that interprets what we perceive.

Whatever we think and feel creates vibrational energy within us; that energy emitted by one person will attract other similar energies at the same or similar vibration or frequency in our environment. Energy travels by vibration, and each emotion emitted by me has a vibrational frequency. The emotion of joy has its own frequency (Fig. 2). The emotion of fear or doubt has a totally different frequency (Fig. 3). Let's say when I am happy, I emit a vibration of joy, happiness, and satisfaction. My energy is high, and I feel good about myself and others around me. The energy frequency that I emit from that joy looks like this (Fig. 2).

Note: Image is a representative visualization for a better understanding only.

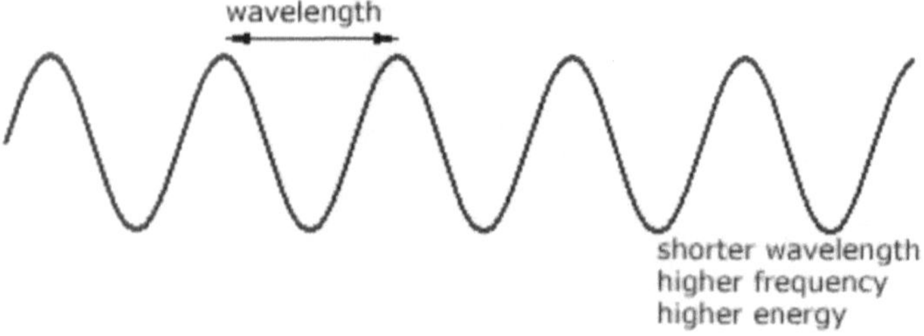

Fig. 2: Wavelength frequency of Happy, Joy, Satisfaction, etc. situated on a **higher** level of the emotional scale *(Courtesy of www.crunchreviews.com).*

On the contrary, if I feel down, sad, worried, and afraid, then the energy I emit from those feelings would look like this (Fig. 3).

Fig. 3: Wavelength frequency of Worry, Doubt, Fear, etc. situated on a **lower** level of the emotional scale *(Courtesy of www.crunchreviews.com).*

We can see that those two wavelengths are not equal. Therefore, they don't match each other, and thus, they cannot attract each other. They are situated at different vibrations and thus vibrate at different energy levels. We know that like attracts like. So, if I am happy, then I am on a high vibe frequency; thus, whoever is happy around me would be attracted to me and I to them, creating synergy that amplifies and turns on the momentum.

The same concept goes when I am feeling fear, doubt, and worry. Those emotions are at the bottom of Abraham-Hicks' emotional scale, and it's the worst place to be in. If people in my environment have that same energy, I will be attracted to them and they to me. A synergy of bad vibes is then created, eventually creating momentum. That was what happened when the World Health Organization declared a pandemic situation for COVID-19 in March 2020. The whole world was living in fear, desperation, and uncertainty. It was collective vibrational fear energy that has been created and has lasted worldwide for a long period of more than two years now (at the time of this writing). Thus, all our fear of death created a momentum of fear energy around the world that has led to the shutdown globally.

But even in that fear and doubt, there are still people who take time to create new ideas, and as we can see, innovation grows everywhere after the pandemic. Those people are in a higher emotional vibe, and thus, they attract more people who are innovative like them to cocreate and bring to the world amazing products that help the advancement of high technology. Thus, there is always the energy of wanted and unwanted in any situation, and each one of us has the choice to choose which end of the stick we want to be on.

Each of us is born on this planet Earth because we are attracted to the energy of this planet. We emit the same energy, and so we are meant to be here. If it had not been for the presence of oxygen on this planet, the animal kingdom and we wouldn't exist. The fact is that oxygen is attracted to this planet; then we are also attracted to the planet because of the existence of oxygen. Thus, everything is created through the order of the Law of Attraction.

REFLECTION: What is the Law of Attraction for you?

State here your definition of the Law of Attraction. What is the ONE thing that you can reprogram in your mind to practice the Law of Attraction every day in order to attract what you want in life?

____

____

____

____

____

____

____

____

____

____

____

____

____

____

____

____

CHAPTER IV

WHY ON PLANET EARTH?

*"When you change the way you look at things,
the things you look at change."*

—Dr. Wayne W. Dyer

Why was I born here and not somewhere else? It's not a coincidence—all is planned according to the alignment of the Universe.

I am attached to planet Earth as it is attached to me. I am at that level of evolution when my desires and energy are in perfect alignment with the creations that are on planet Earth. As the expression "like attracts like" still stands by its premise, the Law of Attraction has no discrimination.

Before coming to planet Earth, I was eager— I wanted to be born, to cocreate with others. The human being is the only species on this planet that requires the longest time to be mature and develop to its full potential because we are emotionally attached and are influenced by others who have been here before us. We are influenced by their thinking and their reactions towards us, and we are shaped and programmed by those conditions without questioning, without being conscious of our purpose before we came here.

From generation to generation, from culture to the thinking of various religions, we are programmed by our parents, relatives, teachers, governments, and the environments where we have been as well as where we are now. Our perceptions are the result of our thinking, our program, and our paradigm. Unless we are conscious of our perceptions, thinking, the definition of life, and the world that we perceive around us, we go on with life by default most of the time.

I am on this planet for a purpose, which is to cocreate with others to create more of what I want, to make a better world according to my desires. I am evaluating and evolving and will expand to become more of who I want to be. So, while I am on this paradise that is our planet Earth, I do my best to bring joy and happiness to myself and to others around me. I cocreate with others for the evolution of mankind. That's the reason why I am here on this planet.

I know that the Law of Attraction brings me to join people who have the same mindset as I do—the people with a desire to thrive, change, help others, and live in joy and happiness. People who are fearless, who have the courage to continue even though they fail so many times. People who want to help others to live in a better world without forcing anyone to do what they want.

When people do what I want them to do, it is because their mission is aligned with mine, and we perceive the task as cocreation instead of perceiving it as an exchange of services. I am on this planet with a purpose—whether I am homeless or the richest woman/man on this planet, and I am here with a purpose to help others to contribute to the evolution of *humanity*.

Whether I am poor or rich, ugly or beautiful, bad or good, etc., I am here with the **purpose** to help others be conscious of their thinking and feelings towards me so that they can become wiser, reprogram their paradigm, change their mindset of what they think is bad, and slowly see the good things in the bad. That is the only way to slowly create what we want in life.

Through love and sympathy for others and through courage and trust that everything happens to me because I attract it, I can make my consciousness work better for me in a way that I want. My existence on this planet is not random. It is by choice; it is because my intention to come here vibrates with the family that I was born in at the moment of my conception. Every creation on this planet Earth starts with an emotional vibration first, then comes into reality so that we can see, hear, touch, smell, taste, and feel with our five senses.

Anything that we see is the leading edge of source energy, and we are energy in its physical form. We are energy that cocreates together to make this world better to live in.

The world is in the process of constant evolution. It changes every day whether we notice it or not, just like the cells in our body change every millisecond. The ones who can notice the change are the ones who are changing. The only way to change is to be **conscious** of one's **feelings** so that when the change starts **from the inside**, then the outside will make its appearance with time. **"I start to change my perceptions within me first; only then will the world's perceptions about me change."** It is only then that I can inspire and influence others for my purpose in life.

Start with me—I change, then my family changes, then my organization changes, then my community changes, then my country changes, then the world changes. Then I can say I inspire others to change for the better. My "just call" is answered, my purpose is accomplished, and my legacy is imprinted in the habits of human beings on planet Earth.

REFLECTION: Be conscious of your thinking.

Practice for thirty days to be conscious (aware) about your thinking and feelings. Every time your mind puts you in a victimization spot, get out of it. Notice your emotions and lower your ego in order to raise your emotional vibrational energy. Write your observations here during the thirty days. You can also share your observations in the consciousness community here: Facebook.com/groups/startwithmeconsciousness.

CHAPTER V

MY PURPOSE IN LIFE

"The meaning of life is to find your gift.
The purpose of life is to give it away."

—Pablo Picasso

What do I want to accomplish on Earth? What do people remember of me when I will no longer be here? What legacy do I want to leave behind? Who am I?

Entering a funeral home, I see all my friends and relatives there—a sense of peace and ecstasy invades me, and people are mourning at a casket. I approach near the front and look into the casket; I see my physical self laying in it. Looking around, I see and hear my friends and relatives talking about me, but they don't see or hear me. I have transitioned into non-physical form and am now witnessing my own departing event from the physical world. Do I like what I hear from those people who talk about me? Or do I find misalignment in my vibrational energy?

They are talking about my physical passage on this planet Earth—what I have done and should have done. Do I agree with what they say, or do I find them exaggerating about me? Then I ask myself, "What good have I done on this planet Earth?"

My purpose in this life is very simple. I came here to spread the words of **peace on Earth** and **love** to all who want to receive it and enjoy paradise on this marvelous planet. That is my purpose. It's up to me to figure out how to do it. If I take one step at a time, one action at a time, and say yes only to opportunities that make me happy and joyful or eager to do, then I know that I am on the right path.

Putting myself in a *happy* position is the key here. Sometimes I do things that do not bring me joy but to please others. This is not good for me if I want to get closer to my purpose. It has to please me and others at the same time. When two or more persons agree to go in the same direction, synergy is created.

When I do things that put me in a resistant mode, I try to be conscious about what makes me feel so, then I decide to continue with that same feeling or not. When I align with my purpose, I feel the eagerness, enthusiasm, and happiness to accomplish what I plan to do. That's where I know that I am accomplishing my mission. Being conscious about what I want and don't want, I can direct my mind to the feeling of what I want so that the Law of Attraction brings me more of that feeling of wanting.

"It's not a matter of what others think about me. It's what I think about me and others that matters to my feelings," and this **"feeling good now"** is the key to putting myself in a position of being more approachable and closer to the vortex, thus leading me to manifest things that I want. What I want is to leave a legacy to the world. What legacy do I want to leave then?

I imagine opening the *Webster's Dictionary* towards the end, looking for my name. I find my name there with a long description beside it.

"Mina Vo: Born in Vietnam and immigrated to Canada in 1980. She was one of the six girls in the Vo family. At the age of fifty-two, her desire was to become a Law of Attraction coach to help others in their self-development endeavor. By 2030, she was known to impact over one billion lives on this planet Earth with her teaching about the Law of Attraction and consciousness via her books that sold millions of copies around the world and were translated into more than fifty languages . . ."

That's how I start from the end and define my purpose in life. That is my legacy. What is yours?

REFLECTION: Start from the end and define your purpose in life.

Now it is your turn to write your biography. Start from the end and create your desired life below. You don't have to show anybody the details about your purpose; you just need to be conscious about it, write it out, take action, and discipline yourself to do it.

CHAPTER VI

MY MISSION STATEMENT

*"If you can't explain it simply,
you don't understand it well enough."*

—Albert Einstein

My purpose is to bring joy and happiness to others around me and always remember to start with me first. Once I know my purpose, then I can sit down and write my mission statement.

Your mission statement is a desire, a goal to be accomplished. It's the action to your purpose in life. It states who you are, your values, and what you stand for. It is simple, concise, and has its reason to be. It doesn't matter who you are—the important thing here is to know your values, why you do what you do, and how you can make an impact on other people's lives.

That impact that you want to make on others is the *why* to your *purpose* in life. That is the drive that makes you wake up every morning and makes you eager to start your day. Then *how* do you make that impact? Finally, describe *who* you are, your values, and what you stand for.

It might take a little time to think about your mission statement, but once you know your purpose and the order of your values and needs, it becomes clear to you about who you are and what you want in order to live a happy life that responds to your needs.

According to the great motivational speaker and author Anthony (Tony) Robbins, there are six fundamental needs that human beings are seeking. It is similar to Abraham Maslow's hierarchy of needs, which are 1) Physiological, 2) Security, 3) Love/Belonging, 4) Esteem, and 5) Self-Actualization. Humans need to reach the basic need starting at level #1 first, which is the Physiological need for survival (breathing, food, and water) before they can feel and think about the following needs, which are Security, Love/Belonging, Esteem, and Self-Actualization. Once you attain your last need, you would then experience a feeling of fulfillment in whatever you do.

Fulfillment is a way of contributing to society. When we are in a position where we can give someone a chance to grow, thrive, and survive, we then feel fulfilled because that is the way we have been taught since we were born. We were being taken care of by our parents who provided us food and shelter for our survival on this planet; once grown up, we just want to do the same for younger generations to prevent the extinction of the human race. It has been programmed in us, and it's an innate character.

Our characters make us who we are according to the needs that we have in our internal world. I find that the six needs defined by Tony Robbins are more detailed, precise, and easier to categorize. Once you understand those needs, you can see where you and others are situated on the scale of needs (Fig. 4).

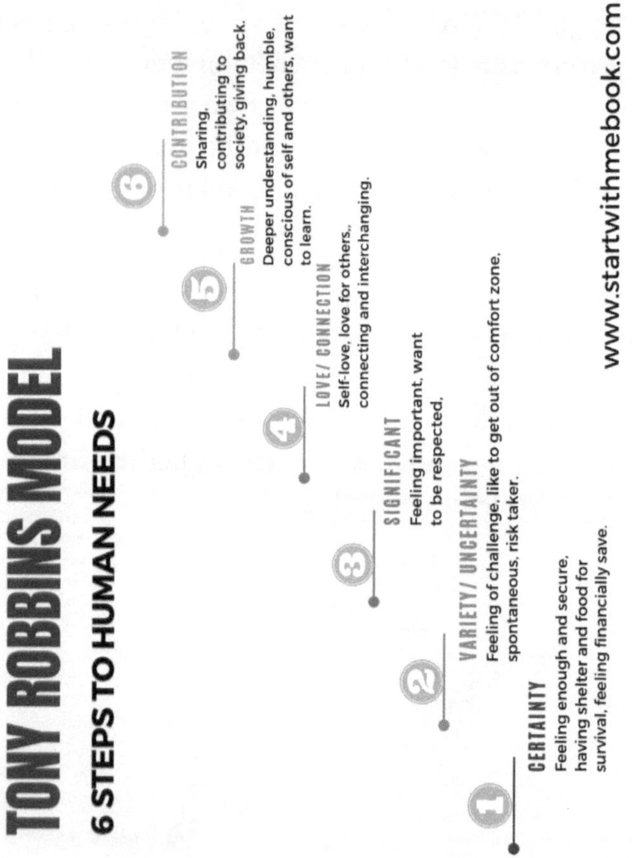

Fig. 4: The six human needs according to Tony Robbins.

Let's look at those needs in detail so that it'll give you an idea of where your needs are met on the scale; you can then determine how to write your mission statement once you know where your needs are and what you want.

The need for:

1. **CERTAINTY**

   If you have the fundamental needs that a person requires to survive, like having food on the table and feeling comfortable financially, you have the basic needs for your survival. If any of these needs are not attainable for you yet, then it's hard for you to seek other needs down the line.

2. **VARIETY/UNCERTAINTY**

   This relates to feeling the drive to do something unusual. Spontaneity does not bother you but drives you to take action, to discover more, and to get out of your comfort zone. You cannot seek variety if your first need is not fulfilled, because if certainty is not attained yet, how can you survive in an uncertain world? People who are stuck here don't grow much.

3. **SIGNIFICANT**

   Everybody wants to feel important; we want appreciation and respect from others. All of us have the need to be seen, be known, and be a celebrity in the eyes of others, relying on the perception of ourselves and others to feed our motivation for fame. Once this is not a need anymore, you become humble with all the admiration from others.

4. **LOVE/CONNECTION**

You need to connect with others to socialize, to share the love and appreciation that you have for them. You appreciate others because you love and appreciate yourself. Once you feel important regardless of others' perceptions of you, then the need for your self-love and loving others is fulfilled. It could also be at the other end where you need to be loved, and you could be seeking love at the wrong place because you are needing too much of it. In this latter case, your need is not yet fulfilled. The need for love is fulfilled when you can independently live and let live—you then manifest the unconditional love.

5. **GROWTH**

When you have the love and appreciation in you, you just feel that you have to learn more and grow—you don't diminish yourself. At this level, you become a person who has the confidence, the assurance to grow and thrive more in your learning. Just like Albert Einstein said, *"The more I don't know, the more I learn; the more I learn, the more I realize that I don't know much."* Once this need is met, which means that you accept being a student all the time, you'll then want to give back to society what you've learned. Here you become more spiritual and more conscious about your feelings, emotions, and vibrational energy. It's the maturity of the mind.

6. **CONTRIBUTION**

   Giving back takes certainty, spontaneity, and feeling significant to connect and grow. Now, since your other needs have been met, the only thing that is left for you is to contribute to society and leave a legacy for the next generations to come. You are here with your *purpose*, your *why*, your *mission*.

In order to write your mission statement, you need to visualize that you have fulfilled all of those needs to the end. The first four needs are physical needs to satisfy your physical being, and the last two are spiritual needs, once the physical needs are fulfilled. Go through those six human needs and try to see which of your needs are already fulfilled and which ones you still need to work on.

If you are not yet at #6, which is CONTRIBUTION, visualize that you are there already, that you are a millionaire right now, without any worry about your health, finance, relationship, society, and so on. You are at peace with yourself and satisfied with who you are and your accomplishments. What do you want to do now after you've got all that you want in life? Start to write out your mission statement below.

Here are some examples of the mission statements for a person who is:

A stay-at-home mom: "Being a great mom to my children and a great wife to my husband by taking care of them and the household. To take care of my family so that everybody will live happily as desired."

A homeless person: "To live day by day so that I can be happy with what I have."

A religious leader: "To create as many followers as possible so that I can align them with my religious thinking."

A farmer: "To be a great farmer so that I can bring delicious fruits and vegetables to the world."

A constructor: "To be a great shelter builder so that people feel secure to live in what I've built."

A great worker: "To be great at what I do and where I am so that my boss is happy with my work. I feel great and my colleagues love my help and enthusiastic presence. I feel that I contribute to my organization."

A great boss: "To understand others and be understood so that I can lead, inspire, and communicate my vision clearly to others in order to help them stand up and thrive for the benefit of all."

A great student: "To be successful in what I am studying so that I can contribute my knowledge, ideas, and creations to the continuous evolution of the world's technology."

An entrepreneur: "To always have the drive, discipline, courage, and tenacity to move forward so that I can reach my goals and inspire others to do the same."

A statement of purpose or mission should start with:

To (contribute) **so that** (impact)[1]

My mission statement is:
Wanting to see people live in a harmonious and prosperous environment by influencing and inspiring them to reach their goals and improve their lives so that they can help themselves and inspire others to do the same for a better contribution to humanity.

---

[1] Ref: *Find Your Why* by Simon Sinek, David Mead, and Peter Docker.

REFLECTION: Your mission statement.

What is your mission statement? Write it down here:

CHAPTER VII

WHAT TO DO WITH MY PURPOSE? BE CONSCIOUS OF THE CHANGE

"Life will only change when you become more committed to your dreams than you are to your comfort zone."

—Billy Cox

Now that you have your mission statement written, what is the next step for you? Are you just writing it down and putting it aside somewhere in a corner of your working desk? Or do you look at it, read it every day, and take action to apply it?

My purpose is to inspire and influence others to become their better selves, to be aware of their consciousness and able to **control their subconscious via their**

consciousness so that they can get what they want in life and inspire others to do the same.

Helping others to get what they want in life helps you to get what you want and be successful. Zig Ziglar said, *"You can have everything in life that you want if you will just help enough other people get what they want."*

Each one of us has the knowledge of something. If we don't take action to share that knowledge with others, we will die with that valuable knowledge buried deep down in our graves. We are born on this planet with a purpose; some of us are conscious of the purpose that we have, and some are not. The purpose of this manuscript is to help the ones who want to be conscious of their purpose and mission so that they can find it, apply it, and live the rest of their life with happiness, serenity, and fulfillment.

Every step of your life has a purpose; when you are a stay-at-home mom, you take care of your kids and your husband; when you are an employee of a corporation, you take care of your responsibilities to do a great job; when you are an entrepreneur, you take care to make your company thrive in order to create more jobs and products that respond to the demand of your customers. In all of those positions, you make sure that you *like* doing it, you *enjoy* doing it, and you have the *passion* to do it. The minute that you are bored and have no passion to do what you are doing, that is the sign that your inner being is telling you to seek other opportunities to do that aligned with your passion and purpose. That's why it is critical and important to write out your statement of purpose, to write out what you want in life, what you want to contribute to society, and what you want to get back in return. Asking someone to sit down and write his or her mission statement is not an easy task to do because most people don't know what they want! Or they know it but don't take action to do things that are required to get what they want.

In Chapter VI, you learned how to write your mission statement. This is very important because this is your *why*, and you have to start with your *why*. Simon Sinek suggests in his book *Start with Why* that your *why* is your *purpose*, your *mission* in life.

Your purpose is what makes you wake up every morning with joy and enthusiasm to go on with your day. Without your purpose in mind, you just wander around like an insect with no destination to go to and no direction to follow. Without your purpose, you go on with life like a person driving to an unknown destination without a GPS. You are 100 percent lost when you go somewhere unknown to you without a map or your GPS, unless someone is showing you the way; and still, there must be trust in that person who shows you the way to ensure that you are on the right path. Life works by the same concept. If you want to become such a person as your mentor or your idol, you have to draw your plan and know which road to take first, which one is second, which one is third, and so on. That's where setting goals is important. But it's no use to set goals and not take action to do them.

If you dream without action, you are just a dreamer. If you set goals without action, you are just a goal setter. If you act without self-discipline, you are just a hard worker. If your discipline is without perseverance, you are just a person who you were before having your dream. You are back to where you were, which is okay if you are happy where you are. Life is always evolving; we are also evolving physically and spiritually. Some evolve faster than others, and that's the way it is.

DREAM + GOALS + DISCIPLINE + ACTION + PERSEVERANCE = The Person I Want to Be

That's the formula for **SUCCESS**.

Whether you are an artist, a homeless person, a worker, a spouse, an entrepreneur, and so on, in each of those roles, you have your purpose in life. If you are happy with where you are, then you know that you are on the right path to your purpose. But if you are not happy with where you are right now, that is the sign from the Universe telling you that there might be a different path you should take or follow in order to bring more happiness into your life.

"The secret to happiness is freedom, and the secret to freedom is courage."

—Thucydides

Everything starts with the right attitude. Let's say you are working in a big corporation right now doing accounting. You love numbers and love the work you are doing, but you don't like the people around you. They don't have the right attitude according to your perception. They talk behind people's backs, and you don't like it. You plan to apply to work for another organization, and luckily you get another accounting job in a new firm. But after a few months of working at the new place, you notice people start to talk behind your back. Then you get bored and annoyed at this new place because people don't align with you, so you start to look for another accounting job somewhere else, and the cycle goes on. You find yourself going around heading from one place to another and thus repeating the cycle again and again. No change at all. Unconsciously, you attract what you think about.

The above scenario is very familiar to most of us who are not conscious of how the Law of Attraction works. This law works by emotions and feelings. Every time you feel something, either good or bad, you attract those energies to you. We are like a radio. We are the receiver and translator at the same time, just like a radio or television. These devices receive and translate messages to us in sounds and pictures. Radios and TVs receive information from a radio or TV station in the form of frequencies. If you want to listen to jazz music, you will turn the knob of your radio to a jazz station, and if you want to listen to classical music, you turn your knob to a classical station in order to hear the music, which receives the frequency and translates that frequency to the sounds of music that you want to hear. The same concept works for a TV, which is a better invention where you can hear and see what has been transmitted at the same time.

Why do I say we are like a radio? Because whatever feelings you are turned to, you would stay in that mood all the time unless you change your mood. There are all kinds of feelings in your surroundings, and each feeling has its own vibrational energy frequency. The feelings of fear, frustration, and sadness are not at the same vibration as the feelings of happiness, joy, and love. So, if you feel that people talk behind your back and you hate them, what you are unconsciously doing is you are turning your knob to the emotion of "hate," so all the vibrations that are related to your feeling of "hate" in your surroundings will attract to you, and the more you think about it and feel it, the more momentum that feeling will create and intensify.

So, when you leave a workplace where you don't like the atmosphere and go to another one, if you still have that feeling of "hate" and "doubt" in your mind, your radar will attract and pull that vibrational energy frequency from your environment even though there is very little of it aimed towards you. If you continue to have that feeling, you will attract it more to you, thus creating a momentum of that feeling eventually. So even though you change your workplace, you are still the same person who has the same thinking, same mindset, same paradigm, and same emotions towards your colleagues and environment, unless you are conscious about your attitude and *ready to change*.

You are UNCONSCIOUSLY and DELIBERATELY creating the same scenario that you either like or don't like. The Law of Attraction does not differentiate which emotion you like and which you don't like. The Law of Attraction just gives you more of what you *feel* by the Law of Vibration. *Like* attracts *like*: just as the molecular law in chemistry is the same as the Law of Attraction.

Knowing how the Law of Attraction works helped me comprehend how to live the life that I want to have and who I want to be. Before deciding on what I want and who I want to be, I have to know my purpose. Once I know my purpose, which is to influence and inspire others, it makes me *conscious* about *who I am* and *what attitude* I can take to become the person I want to be.

This takes time and consciousness (awareness) about my **thinking**, my attitude, or my mistakes. I function by default when I am not aware of my feelings. I go with my paradigm, with what has been programmed in me from zero to seven years old and beyond—what I have learned from my parents and my environment until now. I express it in my thoughts, feelings, and reactions. Since I think and react in a certain way, I attract the same thinking and reactions from others around me in that way. It's the Law of Attraction. Since my thought is vibrational energy, it attracts the same energy that it finds in its environment regardless of the distance and pulls to me that same emotion.

So, let's go back to what to do with your purpose. If your purpose is to be one of the best accountants in your firm in order to serve your clients well, then it is to your advantage to put yourself in a high vibrational energy frequency of loving what you do and appreciating what you have, including people around you, right? If your thoughts always stay at that high frequency, it vibrates around you and attracts more of the same vibrational energy frequency (thought) in your environment, thus creating momentum or synergy.

But if your thought is in a lower vibrational energy frequency on the emotional scale, which is hate, frustration, doubt, sadness, and so on, then the Law of Attraction would bring to you more and more of those feelings from your environment, thus creating momentum and synergy with the same thought.

That's why when you change your environment and are not conscious about changing yourself, you create the same situation as the previous one that you don't like, and the cycle goes on. So, ask yourself, which one is easier to change? Changing your thinking and attitude? Or wanting your environment to change in order to cope with your thinking and attitude?

It is much easier to change yourself than to ask someone else to change for you. But how to change oneself? By being conscious of one's feelings, emotions, and reactions.

You can change the world by *changing yourself one step at a time*. The easiest way to change yourself is by *changing your perception* rather than *expecting* people to *change their perception for you*.

REFLECTION: How can you change to become a better version of yourself?

Write out an unpleasant situation that you encountered and how you reacted to it. How could you do better considering the knowledge you have learned about the Law of Attraction now? How can you change your thinking so that your attitude changes for the better?

CHAPTER VIII

MY NEXT STEP: SETTING GOALS

*"Without goals, and plans to reach them, you are like
a ship that has set sail with no destination."*

—Fitzhugh Dodson

Now that you have found your purpose and know what to do with your *why*, the next step is to work on your plan and take action in order to reach your goals.

A dream without action remains only a dream. To make your dreams come true, you have to take time, with planning, dedication, and perseverance. You can eventually reach your goals and be where you want to be five to ten years from now.

As human nature, we tend to have a grandiose idea at first, then we start the project, but along the line, there are obstacles, the ups and downs of the project; the instant gratification gets in the way, then we get discouraged and slow down, eventually coming to an end with the project that could bring lots of potential if we continue.

That is why knowing your purpose, your *why*, is very important. You know what your purpose is so that every time you encounter hardships and obstacles in life, your mission reminds you of what you are here for, what impact you want to make, and what you should do to thrive and survive to reach where you want to be.

Let's say if you want to become one of the best hockey players in the National Hockey League, you have to first know how to skate, then learn the rules of the game, but the hardest part is to discipline yourself to wake up early every Saturday or Sunday morning to practice with the team, not counting the practice on your own. All those micro steps take time and dedication. You can only be successful if you go through all of those steps and persevere to practice every day, even though some days you don't feel like it. **This is where most people fail and cannot get what they want in life.** It's the lack of **self-discipline**. It's even getting harder to be disciplined nowadays since we have all kinds of distractions around us. Pieces of information are bombarding us from everywhere, and we need to practice focusing intensively on what we want to accomplish for the day.

In order to be self-disciplined, you work with your timer, your pen, and your agenda to write down your short-, medium-, and long-term goals.

To set your goals, you need to know your purpose, where you want to go and to be in one, three, and five years from now. You don't have to share your goals with others, unless you want to be accountable, in order to move forward faster. Let's say you want to be financially free five years from now. Your dream is to create an online business that runs on automation so that you can have free time with your family and friends. You are a digital marketer right now and would like to be successful in your business five years from now. With a pen and a notebook, you sit down and write your goals starting from the end. Before starting, you need to write a list of what is required to be a successful online business owner in your field. These are a few points to think about:

1. Knowledge about the subject, your field of expertise, what you know, and what you need to learn.
2. How to build an online program?
3. How to do online marketing?
4. How to deliver your products or services?
5. How to keep clients coming back to you for more?

All of that information should be spread in a five-year plan if you are a full-time employee right now. It could be a one-year plan if you have almost all of that knowledge—your learning time would be shorter. Once you acquire what you should know and know where to seek further knowledge, then you can plan your goals starting from the end.

Here is an example of a five-year plan:

1. I want to work online everywhere in the world.
2. I want to be financially free, earning $10K to $20K per month.
3. I want to inspire the world with my knowledge.
4. I want my house to be paid off.
5. I want to have a great relationship with my husband/wife and children.
6. I want to have the freedom of choice—to do what I want and where I want it.

This is an ideal life that you might wish to have in five years.

Now you have to work backward again for your plan three years from now. Taking every point of your five-year plan, you want to give more detail to it.

Example:

For #1: **I want to work online everywhere in the world.**

Always in the perspective of teaching your clients how to become an effective digital marketer, here are the questions that you should ask yourself:

i. My knowledge about being an efficient marketer in my field: Do I need to take courses and learn more about it? If not, then I can start to write out the benefits that my clients can get from me.

ii. My knowledge about creating an online program: Where am I now? What should I learn to improve?

iii. My knowledge about online marketing: What are the different ways of online marketing that I can take a look at and choose from?

iv. I want to take action to acquire those bits of knowledge: Where can I go from here?

For #2: **I want to be financially free, earning $10K to $20K per month.**

Again, to be able to earn $10K to $20K per month, what do you need to do as services for the exchange of the amount of money that you want?

You then go on with each and every point that you've written down to be able to see more clearly what you want. Please go to **www.startwithmebook.com/5yp** to download the exercise that will help you to set your goals.

Going through every one of the points above and doing the exercise will help you to see more clearly what you want and need to design a future that you plan to have.

Now that you know your purpose and how to plan your goals, the only thing left to do is to *take action* and *be disciplined*.

REFLECTION:

Don't forget to visit **www.startwithmebook.com/5yp** to download a blueprint to set your five-year-plan goals.

CHAPTER IX

SELF-DISCIPLINE

"Discipline is choosing between what you want
NOW and what you want MOST."

—Abraham Lincoln

Setting goals is easy; planning and taking action are quite easy too. The hard part is the *self-discipline*. Without self-discipline, there wouldn't be a Picasso, a Beethoven, an Elon Musk, a Steve Jobs, a Jeff Bezos, a Mark Zuckerberg, an Oprah Winfrey, a Larry Page, a Sergey Brin, a Celine Dion and many more renowned celebrities on this planet.

Self-discipline is not easy. If it was, then everyone would have what they want in life by the time they are set to receive it. To get what you want, you have to discipline yourself to get into the habit of doing what you plan to do every day, even though some days, you don't feel like doing it.

There are many things in your life that you don't feel like doing. For example, making phone calls, prospecting, selling, building a side business in the evenings and working full-time during the day, and so on. But you take time and discipline yourself to do them anyway because you know that there is a reward for you to enjoy down the road.

Before knowing how to discipline yourself, you've got to know **what you want**— your goals and desires. Then, classify them in the **"I MUST HAVE FUN to DELEGATE and ELIMINATE"** system below.

I MUST = Important and **MUST do** tasks—serious consequences for non-completion.

Things that **you must do** even though you don't feel like doing them. Your stream of income for you or your business will be affected if you don't take action or don't have the discipline to do them regularly every day.

For example:

- Going to work every day.
- Making phone calls to potential clients to sell.

HAVE = HAVE to do tasks—mild consequences for non-completion.

Things that you **have to or should do** and that take time to do. This will bring more income to you or your business; it's the extra mile that you decide to take on to differentiate yourself from everybody else in your field of expertise.

For example:

- Taking the initiative to do more at work to make yourself stand out and be different from others. Leaders are always spotted by the work they do and the contributions they make.

- Following up with clients to close a sale. Just to tell you how important it is: one of my real estate agents got a sale when he did his follow-up with me on a deal that I had forgotten. So, it is worth the effort to go the extra mile.

FUN = FUN to do—no consequences for non-completion.

Things that you feel good doing. They do not directly affect your work or your business, but they feel good to do and they make you and others around you feel happy and replenished. When you feel happy, you put yourself on a high vibrational energy frequency; thus, it helps you to become more productive and constructive.

For example:

- Going out for a walk or taking time with family. It doesn't affect your business if it's not done, though it's fun to do and it boosts up your morale.

DELEGATE = DELEGATE what is possible to do—have someone do the job better and faster than you.

You can be great at one thing but not great at everything. For things that you're not great at, it's better to get someone who has more experience or expertise than you to do it. Sometimes, it's not a matter of expertise; it's a matter of having more time so that you can concentrate on strategic thoughts for your life or business. Delegation takes trust, so you have to trust those persons in order to let them do things that you want them to do for you. People who cannot delegate are the ones who either have a hard time trusting someone else or are too shy to ask for help. It's a matter of mindset and paradigm.

For example:

- Hiring contractors or freelancers to accomplish a task.
- Asking for help at work.

ELIMINATE = ELIMINATE things that are unimportant and that waste your time.

Eliminate all things that waste your time. Before making a decision to do an activity, get into the habit of asking yourself these questions: Is this action going to help me in the advancing of my project, calling, cause, and so on? Would it help me to bring more money to my business? Would it be helpful for my personal development? If the answer is no to the above questions, then you know where to concentrate your time most and where not to.

For example:

- Poking around on social media for gossip.
- Saying negative things about others.
- Having a bad attitude towards others.
- Telling people what to do when they don't need any of your opinions.

Those activities should be out of your agenda because they don't serve you well in the advancement of your purpose. Set priorities and put important tasks to do first even though they are not urgent. Urgency might put you in the mode of putting out fire all the time and thus create the energy of being overwhelmed, which is a low vibrational energy frequency.

Learn to organize your tasks and categorize them in order of importance to help discipline yourself to be more productive. To acquire self-discipline, you have to divide your goal into **micro steps**.

For example, if you want to lose twenty pounds, you have to take the time to exercise for thirty to sixty minutes each day with the right coach and the right tools. If you work out nights and days combined with good eating habits and follow the guidance of your coach, you'll soon get to the size that you want.

To make \$5K to \$10K per month in your business, you have to plan the steps that you have to take to get there—it's your map, your GPS. The hard part is to do it **consistently** every day; that is what we call **self-discipline**.

Let's say if I want to finish writing this book following a particular timeline, I have to divide the book into milestone subjects, then put them into chapters. If I want to finish my thirteen chapters in four months, then I have to finish at least three and a quarter chapters each month. I then set to write one chapter per week. Now, how much time do I have per week to put on my writing? I have only two hours of free time per week. Then, I have to finish writing each chapter in two hours of my free time. That is one of my micro steps. The next step is to find an editor, then a publisher, and so on until my book will be launched. But then I must continue the marketing for my book in order for it to continue selling if I want to inspire and help those who align with my philosophy and have earnings at the same time.

My macro goal is to have the book continue to sell forever, but I have to discipline myself every day in order to build my plan, my system, and get the momentum going.

Self-discipline is not to be done for a day or two. It is a continuous process that lasts for a lifetime. Because once we reach our goal, we set another one. Since we are creators, we always want to create more. So, discipline for each project is a habit, and once the habit is acquired, we do it automatically without thinking, just like driving a car and talking to someone at the same time. Once you get it, the habit is acquired, and the discipline is set.

According to Elbert Hubbard, one of the most prolific writers in the American history of literature, *"Self-discipline is the ability to make yourself do what you should do when you should do it, whether you feel like it or not."*

Another legend in the field of success and achievement, Kop Kopmeyer once talked to Brian Tracy and stated: *"There are 999 other success principles that I have found in my reading and experience, but without self-discipline, none of them work. With self-discipline, they all work."*

Self-discipline is a skill that can be learned. Once a skill becomes a habit, then self-discipline is acquired. Self-discipline unlocks your innate power to achieve. Your talent, education, and intelligence are not the sole keys to success. Without self-discipline, all the talents or chances in the world won't lead you to where you want to be. It is a skill that can be learned, but most people don't take the time to learn it; they would rather take time to be around the playground of social media where most of their time is wasted on unimportant facts.

To practice self-discipline, you have to set out what you want—your goals and objectives. When do you want to get what you want? What is required from you to achieve what you want?

I find that I can discipline myself easier when I set the timer to do certain tasks that I planned to do during the day. It forces me to finish the task in that time frame. If the timer is not on, I might take more time to finish the task that I've planned to do because of distractions. So, **setting the timer** for each task and the **deadline** for each macro and micro step helps me to discipline better.

REFLECTION: Be conscious to apply self-discipline in your life.

1. Write out what prevents you from becoming a self-disciplined person.

____

____

____

____

2. Do you know anyone who is **the worst self-disciplined** person in your opinion? Describe the person and state how you feel when you encounter that person.

____

____

____

____

3. List all the feelings you experience when you are self-disciplined.

____

____

____

____

4. **Choose one habit** that you want to discipline yourself for thirty days. Once the first habit is acquired, choose another one, and so on until all your actions become habits.

   For example, wanting to wake up at 5:00 am so that you have more time to do what you want.

CHAPTER X

MY STEPS TOWARDS MY DESIRES

"The journey of a thousand miles begins with a single step."

—Lao Tzu

To get what I want, I must discipline myself every minute, every hour, and every day to get into the habit of reaching my goal. I have found my purpose, I planned my journey to respond to my purpose, I take action according to my plan, and most of all, I discipline myself with perseverance.

Every step that I take, there is the up and down, certainty and doubt, joy and sadness; it's a mix of emotions. The challenge is to keep going even in my down, doubtful, and worrisome periods. I know that in those moments,

I was going against the current, and I was thinking with my own old paradigm, but those moments have to happen in order for me to recognize, realize, and be conscious of what I want.

My sense of purpose helped me to focus and say no to any event or demand from my environment that was not aligned with my purpose. I used to say yes to everything that came to me by default via the Law of Attraction. This is because I had no purpose—I didn't know what I wanted, so the Universe just threw at me whatever had similarities to my alignment. I function by default. It's up to me to position myself to receive it or not.

If I know what my purpose is, I set my goal to reach what I want, and then I know what to do each day to get focused. Every event that comes to me that makes me lose my time and focus would be put aside. Knowing what I want helps to put me into laser focus on what I want to reach, even though I have many projects going on. Every one of them is to help inspire people and help them be conscious about what they want in order to reach their goals and improve their lives so that they can inspire others to do the same for a better contribution to humanity.

I always wanted to be a teacher to help others to know more about themselves so that they can have what they want in life. Once they know about their desires, they will take action to create the life that they want to have and have a good mindset to inspire others to do the same. It's important for me to write my mission statement out on a piece of paper so that it reminds me all the time who I am and what I am here for.

Of course, sometimes my actions and my thinking can upset others, and that's okay for me. The important thing is that I feel good about my decision. Others have their own perceptions. I cannot please everyone; otherwise, I would live for them and not for me, so I would be out of alignment all the time, which will eventually lead me into a situation of unhappiness, frustration, and so on. That's something I don't want.

To get what I want, what do I need? A pen and a notebook. I just write down what I want and set a deadline to do it. It sounds like setting goals, doesn't it? Yes, it definitely does! Now, it's time to get into action!

The steps towards your desires are very simple.

FIRST STEP:

Know your purpose—what you want in life, your mission statement, your dream, your inspiration, your passion, your contribution. Everybody wants to be financially free and have the freedom to choose and do what they want in life, but not many people can reach that level of freedom. When you write your mission statement with a financially free mindset, the question that you ask yourself when you write it out is: Now that I have everything I want in terms of health, finance, love, and so on, what do I want to do in order to contribute to society? In other words, "What do I want to do now that I am financially free?"

SECOND STEP:

Find a project that motivates and inspires you—something that can keep you going even in hard times. Take Elon Musk and Jeff Bezos—both have the desire to populate the human race outside of our planet Earth, and they are working on developing technologies for that. If you are a secretary, a doctor, or a janitor, you would want to ask yourself: What are the actions and thinking you can act on now that can make you and others happy at the same time?

REFLECTION: Setting macro and micro steps.

1. Have a pen and a notebook. Write down ONE ACTION you want to take that can change and improve your life a month from now—your goal.

____

____

____

____

____

2. What are the steps that are needed for you to get there? Write down your macro steps.

____

____

____

____

____

3. From each macro step, write down the micro steps that you need to take every day in order to accomplish each of your micro steps. Ask yourself if you have enough time allotted to accomplish those steps in that time frame.

Macro step I:

____

____

Micro steps:

1. ____

____

____

____

2. ____

____

____

____

Macro step II:

____

____

Micro steps:

1. _____________________________________

____

____

____

2. _____________________________________

____

____

____

Continue on with each macro step.

4. Set a deadline to accomplish each macro step. You can give yourself a little compensation every time you reach your micro step on time. That will encourage you to go on and achieve each step with eagerness and motivation.

____

____

____

____

____

____

CHAPTER XI

HOW TO INSPIRE PEOPLE AROUND ME?

*"Let things flow naturally forward in whatever
way they like."*

—Lao Tzu

Now that I know who I am, what my purpose is, what I want, and how to set my goal and get what I want, then what's next? I have to go back to my calling, my *why*, my *purpose*. Why do I want to become a doctor, a dentist, a nurse, a businessperson, a carpenter, a delivery person, or a janitor? Why have I chosen this or that career? What leads me to where I am now? Am I happy where I am now? Or do I need to change?

If I am happy where I am now, then it's easy to know how to inspire others. I only need to be my authentic self, allowing my strengths and weaknesses to be expressed, allowing myself to make mistakes and learn from them. I have to be humble and joyful, allowing people to have their own opinion and allowing myself to have mine, allowing agreement and disagreement.

Remember, to allow is not to tolerate—these are different in vibrational energy frequencies. When you are allowing is when you let people have the freedom of choice; they can think what they want with their own perceptions. Their perception is based on their thinking and paradigm. So, you are not letting their perception affect your mood or your well-being. **You are who you are**—you have your own paradigm and perception. People who have the same thinking as you will definitely align with you, and people who do not won't align with you, and that would be okay too. To tolerate is more of giving people the permission to affect your mood and feelings; it's not the same energy as allowing.

You are not here to tell anyone what to do or what you think. If you do, then you will cause resistance in their emotions, and according to the Law of Attraction, everything that bothers you, you will attract more of it. You have the choice to do whatever you want to in this world. You can choose to be happy, to go with the flow, and to forgive and forget, or to be unhappy, frustrated, anxious, vengeful, and so on. The choice is yours. Now, most people would say: "I don't have a choice." This is because they don't take the time to choose; if they do, they definitely have choices.

Once you learn the steps towards your desire, then you just have to take action in order to be where you want to be. If you want to be a nurse and you love your job because you help others to heal, lighten their pain, and recover, it's a vocation and you love it. Then whenever you spread the love, energy around it attracts more people who are then aligned with you. But if you are a nurse and you're always tired, you don't like what you do, and those sick people annoy you, then your negative energy would spread frustration, hatred, and impatience—thus, you would attract more of those energies around you and create momentum. When you are in that mood, you cannot inspire others. Your negative emotions would repel the positive emotions around you. So that's why you attract more of what you feel. Remember, like attracts like—that's what it means!

To inspire others around you, you need to just be conscious of your emotions, attitudes, and reactions towards others. When you spit in the air, it falls down on your face; it's the law of gravity. When you emit negative energy from you, it attracts negative energy around you; it's the Law of Attraction.

If you want to inspire and influence others, you have to spread positive energy around you all the time. Of course, there are days where things are not going the way you want them to be; you just tell yourself that there are worse moments than that, then switch your mind very fast to get yourself in a better emotional position than a few seconds ago. Continue to do it again and again until you feel good about the situation—that's where you know that you are getting back into your vortex. You can only inspire others when you are aligned with your inner being, with your **source**. Because it's only then that whatever you do, say, or act in an authentic way will spread out to your environment.

You are not asking others to change to make you happy. **You are the only one who can make you happy by changing your thinking about others**. It is much easier to do it that way; otherwise, you would be controlled by the words, emotions, and reactions of others, and so you would be living for others by default and not creating the happy life that you want.

Do not demand your spouse, children, friends, relatives, boss, or colleagues to be who you want them to be. It's very hard to ask all of those people to align with you and your thinking. It is much easier for you to let go of their thoughts that are not aligned with yours and still give them **unconditional love** and appreciation; it is only then that you know you are aligned with your inner being, your source of energy, your God in you, and it is only then that you can inspire others to become better versions of themselves. Once they can slowly transform and get into a more positive vibration, then they will attract more of what they want in life with their unconditional love. You can then say that you have contributed to the change in someone to make this world a better one to live in by taking one action at a time, thus inspiring one person at a time.

Anytime you have a negative thought about yourself or others, switch your mind to an image of a person you want to be in the future. Do you want to be a grumpy person or one with a high emotional quotient? Then, you decide to get onto a higher vibrational energy frequency or stay at that same vibration—it is your choice. You can be inspired, or you can inspire others. The latter will put you more in a position of an influencer who can make an impact on millions of lives. The choice is entirely yours. Be like water—adaptable and shaping yourself to the environment where you are instead of asking your environment to change for you, which is likely impossible to be done. Be with the current because nothing that you want is upstream; everything you want is downstream. You'll get what you want by getting rid of all resistance that is in your way by eliminating negative thoughts and focusing on the positive ones, **the ones that make you feel good**. Just go with the flow—you'll be where you want to be in no time.

REFLECTION: Practice being conscious about your negative thinking and change it to positive thinking.

For the next thirty days, be **conscious** of your negative thinking towards yourself and others. Put an elastic around your wrist—every time a negative thought pops up in your mind about you or other people, be conscious to pull out the elastic and let it go. The snap of the elastic on your wrist will remind you to be conscious about your thinking. Write down your observations about the change you've made after thirty days.

CHAPTER XII

I JUST BE MYSELF, BE AUTHENTIC

"Knowing others is intelligence; knowing yourself is true wisdom. Mastering others is strength; mastering yourself is true power."

—Lao Tzu

How to be myself? I don't want to hurt others; I want them to love me. I need appreciation, I need love, I need compassion, I need people to sympathize with me. I want to belong to them and them to me.

We all want to belong to a group, associate with others, love, and be loved. This is because since we were born, we were taught to obey the rules, to not do things that our parents thought were too dangerous for us to embark on, and to do things that our parents wanted us to do; otherwise, we would receive consequences. We were confined and programmed into our subconscious mind that we have to obey, to please others, and to do what they want us to do; non-obedience could lead to consequences that might be fatal to our existence.

Ours is the only species that requires many years of existence from the day we were born to the day that we are independent enough to take care of ourselves. Some of us only take a few years, like seven or eight, to be independent—some take a lifetime, and most of us take around forty to fifty years—and still, there is a variation of time according to each culture and the environment we live in.

Contrary to the animal or plant kingdoms, we depend on adults to survive from the minute we are born. All animals and plants are left to be independent once they are created on this planet. They don't have as many caring emotions as humans do, so they just let nature take care of their offspring once they have done their job of reproduction. A human child needs the care of a grown-up person in order to survive until he/she is able to eat and find food by themselves. We are still dependent on our environment, our parents, or any adult who takes care of us.

Since we rely on a grown-up to take care of us, we have to follow their rules for our survival; any rebellious act could lead to consequences that we don't want to be imposed upon us. So, we were programmed since birth to think like the ones who took care of us—our parents, guides, relatives, teachers, government, and so on. We follow their rules, and we do what they want us to do, even though sometimes we don't like it. We were programmed to please others first before pleasing ourselves, and we were programmed not to be selfish but to care for others, even though we don't like their opinions and emotions towards us; otherwise, we wouldn't receive the love and appreciation that they have for us.

We were conditioned and programmed in conditional love. The love where IF we do things that please the ones who took care of us, then we would receive their appreciation in return, but if we don't do what they would like us to do, then the punishment could be implied.

We were not taught to have **unconditional love**, the love where our parents would love us anyway even though we do things that would bring frustration, fear, and anxiety to them. We cannot blame our parents because they don't know what they don't know. They were taught that way by their parents and ancestors. It is passed down from generation to generation. We are grateful for their teaching and guidance—without our parents and guidance, we couldn't have survived to this day. All of that is just because we care as human beings.

When we care too much, unknowingly, we can deprive someone of his/her freedom of choice, and freedom is what all of us want in the end, isn't it? We work for our financial freedom, the freedom to love and be loved, the freedom to choose. When we are conscious of this freedom to live and let live, we then become independent individuals whom we respect and appreciate, ourselves and others, and only then, we can be ourselves.

How can I be myself? I am myself when I know what I want and what others want. When I know what I want, I can explain and express my feelings, intentions, and thoughts clearly and calmly to others. At the same time, when I know what others want, it will help me to be conscious in choosing my words so that I don't introduce any resistance to others' thoughts.

"Everything can be said; it depends how you say it," rightly says my husband, Claude, and it's so true! My purpose is to inspire others, not to get others to be angry at me. If they disagree with me, that's their perception, and it's okay with me.

I used to be very bossy, telling others what to do and thinking my idea was the best. My ego was very high; I was not aware of that because I didn't have the knowledge that I have today. The knowledge of consciousness, inner being, the Infinite Intelligence, the Law of Attraction, and the laws of the Universe.

Now I am conscious most of the time about my thinking, feeling, and speaking. I express myself more clearly about what I want. When my idea or thinking does not align with someone else's, I would say: "We are not aligned with this thinking. Let's not go this way now. I respect your opinion, and I'm not trying to align you with my opinion, so I demand the same from your part." Then, I stop talking. If the other person tries again to impose his or her opinion, I just smile, look at him or her, and say nothing. My smile soothes the other being, and slowly we enter into a higher vibrational energy frequency, which is love, compassion, and comprehension via communication.

Being myself is reprogramming myself to be a better version of myself. It's a journey to be conscious and to change. I have to be **aware of who I am** and what program or paradigm I had before I can fix myself and reprogram my paradigm, my habit. Once the new habit is acquired, then I have my new paradigm and new thinking; that's where people see the maturity in me, the authentic me.

To be authentic is to be myself, to be able to express my thinking and opinions, even though I know that my thinking may not align with others around me, and to do it in a way that would introduce the least resistance to others. When I don't express myself and confine myself with whatever opinion or act that others want me to do, I then put myself in a position of unhappiness, frustration, and angriness. And so, the more I stay in that situation, the more I attract that kind of energy around me, and thus, momentum is created at that level of vibrational energy, which I don't want.

When people change jobs and still have that frustrated energy from their last job, they come to the new environment with some of that low vibrational energy and, hence, attract more of those who vibrate to that low energy. When you see people who change mates and often attract a similar kind of person in the following relationship, it's because they carry with them all the frustration, angriness, and unhappiness from their ex inside of them. What happened is that, unknowingly, they spread out that vibrational energy frequency around them and attract other people who have the same energy. Thus, nothing changes, unless they change themselves by changing their attitudes and feelings towards the ones that they don't love or appreciate.

Let's say that you were having a bad relationship with someone and have ended your relationship. You are looking for another soulmate. When you separate from your ex, you still have that angry emotion towards him because he is greedy, he beats you, he says bad things about you to others, he wants to have everything for himself, and he left you nothing. How do you feel about it? You would feel hatred, unfairness, and unsatisfaction, right? And those emotions stick with you as long as the other person is still alive. Then you try to find a mate who is better than him, who will love you and share with you the happy moments and also the sad ones, who will take care of you and bring you joy—those are your desires. But do you really feel it when you see your ex in your mind, who didn't give you any happiness, because you haven't forgiven him yet for what he did to you? Then what happens? You are always in that same vibrational energy of lack and hatred, then you attract to you more of what you are lacking, the unhappiness, and so on. The minute someone is presented to you by the Universe, you like his physical appearance, and he seems to take care of you and love you. But a few months down the road, he either shows out his negative energy that repels you or he has too much positive energy that repels the negative energy that is mainly still inside of you at that moment. Then you decide to end the relationship because of too many differences between you and him, and a discordance of vibrational energy frequency appears in your new relationship. You then decide to end this one also, and so the cycle begins and continues. Unconsciously, you were creating relationships that you don't want to have. The only way to get out ahead of it is to forgive and forget. Just go with the flow; live and let others live without constraint or condition. **Focus on the things that you want instead of the things that you don't want**. The more you talk about what you don't want, the more you'll attract to you the things that you don't want.

You are not here to respond to the needs of others and vice versa. You are here to cocreate with them. You are not doing any service to them if you think they need you. The minute that you think they need you, you make them dependent on you, thus introducing the *lack* instead of the *have* into their subconscious mind, and that does not serve them well. Your purpose in life is to make the ones you interact with be independent. Sadly enough, there are people who want others to be dependent on them so that they can control others by their will.

The will to do what I want is the freedom to choose. To be myself, I have to **know what I want** first, then be conscious of my emotions and feelings about what I am asking for. When I am clear enough to know what I want, I can ask life to give it to me with the BELIEF that I already have what I asked for. Everything that I want is already delivered by the Universe; I only have to put myself in the right position to receive it.

But how to position myself to receive it? Just find a **good feeling** place all the time. What **you want** makes you **feel good**, and what you **don't want** makes you **feel bad**. You have the freedom to choose. You have the choice to feel good or bad. Don't let others control your mood, don't let their sayings affect your morale, don't put your nose in others' business, and don't introduce any resistance to your feelings by thinking about what you don't want. Always think about what you want and be happy with what you have now. Don't compare and don't be jealous—just feel good wherever you are with whatever you do. If things are not going the way you want them to go, be **conscious** that it's the message from the Universe telling you to recalibrate your mood and know what you want.

When you are at a place that you don't want to be at, either you continue to do what you are doing there with joy and, at the same time, find a way to get out of it if you don't enjoy it so that you can be in another joyful place, or you just change places. Either way, make sure that you feel good doing it and that you don't introduce any resistance to your emotions or feelings. That's the secret to positioning yourself to receive what you are asking for.

The secret is to know what you want first—life will try to bring you opportunities similar to what you feel, whether your feeling is negative or positive. If life brings you an opportunity that you don't like, it's up to you to accept it or reject it. If you accept it, you must do it with joy and passion; otherwise, you'll always stay in that vicious circle, and you cannot get out of it. If you don't accept the opportunity, then what are the consequences? When you are conscious about what you want and believe that you can achieve it, the choice is easier to make and it's easier for you to decide to say yes or no to an event, a situation, or an opportunity that is presented to you. It's the art of focusing.

Being myself is knowing who I am, what I want, and creating an environment where I have many choices to choose from. But, in order to have many choices, I have to become independent, and I have to bring up my values. The more values I have in me, the more I am in demand for my services, and thus I have choices to attract the people who are aligned with me.

REFLECTION: Practice being yourself by knowing who you are and what you want.

To practice being yourself and to know yourself, here are some situations or questions that you can ask yourself so that you practice making decisions according to your wants:

1. Are you happy where you are right now? If not, state why.

____

____

____

____

____

2. List all the things that don't make you happy in your relationships, work, and health:

RELATIONSHIP	WORK	HEALTH

3. What can you do to change those unhappy situations? **Yes, you have the choice. You just have to think.**

____

____

____

____

How to just be yourself?

- Know what you want. Say yes to any occasion or demand that arrives to you from your environment that aligns with what you want. Know how to say no to any others who do not align with you.

- Do not be afraid to speak out any sincere opinion when people ask you.

- Be authentic and communicate with your positive feelings. Be conscious of your negative feelings and abstain from saying them.

- Anytime you feel negative, you know that you are in a resistant mode. However, knowing what you don't want helps you to know what you do want and reaffirms it to others in order to be back to yourself.

- Always communicate either verbally or emotionally in a non-resistance mode, either with yourself or with others.

- These habits will help you to change your paradigm, making you conscious about who you are and what you want so that you can be back in alignment with your inner being, your soul, the one that has always been in this with you since the beginning of time. Only in that state do you know you are back to who you are meant to be.

CHAPTER XIII

I AM BACK TO WHO I AM MEANT TO BE

*"Service to others is the rent you pay
for your room here on Earth."*

—Muhammad Ali

I am back to my purpose, my mission in this Universe and on this planet Earth.

My mission is to be myself, to understand myself first, to know who I am and where I come from, and then to communicate what I know, my thinking, and my perceptions to others without obligating others to adhere to my thinking or doctrine.

I have been reacting to my environment with my old paradigm, my program that has been installed in me since I was born. This program has been taught to me by my ancestors, parents, teachers, government, and the environment I grew up in. I have been using this old program of mine by default. No one is to blame, and it's nobody's fault—my parents have taught me the best they could, and they cannot teach me what they don't know, right? They did the best they could with the knowledge that they had at that moment. I am grateful for their teaching, their guidance, and their nurturing and caring since I was born. No matter what happened, I know that they always have that caring love for me.

Now that I am conscious of my program, I am cleaning up my hard disk. I keep what is good and let go of what does not serve me anymore, building my mind, my house with a solid foundation, a foundation that knows where it sits, on solid rock so that the house I build now cannot be destroyed by any means. That house vibrates consciousness energy throughout its entire space; those rays of **divine energy** are passing through the opening windows of my house. It is via those windows, **my eyes**, **my soul's windows**, that I observe the beautiful world outside of me.

Through those windows, I create my perceptions of myself and the world—through them, my perceptions translate into emotions, feelings, actions, and reactions. Communication is then established from the inside, within me, to the outside, my environment, and my world.

To be able to translate my perception of the world well so that my communication is effective, I have to be conscious of my program and my paradigm. Once consciousness is installed, the reprogramming process starts; thus, new habits accumulate and become a new paradigm, a new program, a new me.

I am back to **where I am meant to be,** back to **pure source energy** that I am a part of, the energy that we are all a part of—we are ONE from the creator of the Universe. Each one of us is an extension, a branch of that energy in physical form. We are the same in spiritual form, thus different in physical form. We are brothers and sisters with different abilities, mindsets, and paradigms so that we can cocreate with each other with the union of pure energy, our source, the **Infinite Intelligence.**

The life that each one of us has experienced in this world is unique to each and everyone. The ones who are similar attract each other in the vibrational world, and together, they create momentum, either good or bad. The power of choice is vested in each individual, and it is what it is. It is life on Earth, it is WHO I AM, and it STARTS WITH ME.

ACKNOWLEDGEMENTS

I have been raised to be grateful to people who help me in all spheres of my life. Gratitude to everything that the Universe delivers to me. Opportunities, people, connections, and relations—everything is about alignment within myself and others. This book wouldn't have been realized without the excellent work from the Hasmark Publishing team. From the founder, Judy O'Beirn, who took time to listen to my needs, to Michaela Pitman and Ashley Constant (the wonderful publishing assistants), to Mary-Kate Luke for guiding me with AR features, to Kelly Vurinaris for the marketing advice, and of course, to my editor, Harshita Sharma, and my proofreader, Day Bulger, for their great editing work! I am deeply indebted to all of you.

Many thanks to my family and the people I have encountered in my life. Whether you are the ones who make me mad or happy, all of you are there in my life for one reason: to make me consciously aware of my thinking in order to help me grow and become a better version of myself. I call it cocreation, and I'm grateful for your presence in my life. I am the person I am today because of all of you.

Last but not least, thanks to my three young adults from whom I've learned to be a happy mom, and of course, to my wonderful husband with whom I've learned to grow and to be independent—and most of all, « mon amour » Claude, thanks for being patient and supportive throughout all my crazy projects. I would not be who I am today without you.

ABOUT THE AUTHOR

Mina is a Law of Attraction Coach who specializes in Personal Growth, Self-Confidence, Relationship, Leadership and Career Transformation coaching. Her passion is helping entrepreneurs and career women to find their purpose in life.

She serves as a private coach working with a broad spectrum of clients. In addition to being a professional Transformation Coach, she has also presented nationally to general audiences, speaking on the topics of Goal Setting with the Law of Attraction concepts and processes.

She is a collaborative, solution-focused Transformational Coach. Through this approach, she provides support and practical feedback to help clients effectively address personal life challenges. She also integrates coaching techniques and helpful assignments to offer highly personalized programs tailored to you and your needs and requirements. With compassion and understanding, she works with you to help build on your strengths and attain the personal growth you are committed to achieving.

Seeing her clients' evolution, their mindset change, their personal growth expanding to better themselves, and how they are taking actions to become the leaders of their lives makes her feel blessed. Mina is also a co-author with Brian Tracy and other renowned entrepreneurs around the world for *The One Big Thing*, a book about personal development and tricks and tips on marketing, sales, and leadership.

Knowing that her work can help someone who might influence others to become better with their positive attitude and mindset, to become more conscious about their strengths and weaknesses so that they can help themselves and others around them to live harmoniously with each other, she can then say:

"My mission is accomplished."

Mina's Mission:
"Wanting to see people live in a harmonious and prosperous environment by influencing and inspiring them to reach their goals and improve their lives so that they can help themselves and inspire others to do the same for a better contribution to humanity."

Do you want to know What's your next Big Thing is?

The Celebrity Experts in this book have experienced success in many areas. Their advice reflects *The One Big Thing* that made them successful and may do the same for you.

Download your **FREE** copy now!

www.MinaTheOneBigThing.com

To learn more about Mina's work, please visit:
www.minavocoaching.com

With every donation, a voice will be given to the creativity that lies within the hearts of our children living with diverse challenges.

By making this difference, children that may not have been given the opportunity to have their Heart Heard will have the freedom to create beautiful works of art and musical creations.

Donate by visiting

HeartstobeHeard.com

We thank you.